COMPULSORY
SCHOOLING
DISEASE

How children absorb fascist values

Chris Shute

Educational Heretics Press

Published 1993 by Educational Heretics Press, 113 Arundel Drive, Bramcote Hills, Nottingham NG9 3FQ

British Library Cataloguing in Publication Data
Shute, Chris
Compulsory schooling disease: how children absorb fascist values
I. Title
371.5
ISBN 0-9518022-2-4 ✓

Design and production: Community Works, Milton Keynes

Printed by Stanley L Hunt (Printers) Ltd, Rushden, Northamptonshire

COMPULSORY
SCHOOLING
DISEASE

Other publications by the Educational Heretics Press

Unfashionably unfascist? A selection of quotations on education
Compiled by Roland Meighan 1991

Lifelines: a collection of quotations about life and learning
Compiled by Ron Biggs 1992

Forthcoming:
The theory and practice of regressive education
Roland Meighan

Educational Heretics Press exists to question the dogmas of
schooling and education.

Contents

Foreword

Our chief educational problem is deschooling school, rather than deschooling society. Or as John Holt put it, to make schools less like schools. Only then can we begin to cope with the problem Winston Churchill identified in writing to his Minister of Education in 1944:

'Schools have not necessarily much to do with education ... they are mainly institutions of control where certain basic habits must be inculcated in the young. Education is quite different and has little place in school.'

Schools as currently organised on an adult-imposed day-prison model, set up for children a triple tyranny. The first is that of the National Curriculum, a massive exercise in adult chauvinism that Professor Frank Smith has described as the Berlin Wall of Education. A Polish visitor—a member of the Solidarity Education Commission and a Professor in Comparative Education—said she would be reporting back to Poland that the National Curriculum was totalitarian. She saw it from the same stable as the national curriculum of Stalin, or Hitler, or Tito. Poland has experienced two of these in living memory so she should be able to recognise the signs.

The second tyranny is the unwritten curriculum, also known as the hidden curriculum. The unwritten curriculum carries the long-term, permanent messages, many of them identified by Postman and Weingartner in their writings, including:

- Passive acceptance is preferable to active criticism.
- Discovering knowledge is not a task for pupils.
- Recall and regurgitation are the highest forms of intellectual achievement suitable for pupils.
- The voice of authority is to be automatically obeyed.
- The feelings of pupils are irrelevant.
- Education consists of memorising the provided Right Answers.
- Competition is more important than co-operation.
- Helping others always gives way to getting on oneself.
- Writing and reading are more important than talking and thinking.

■ Men are more important than women.

■ Dogma is more desirable than doubt.

No teacher I know sets out to teach these by design, except perhaps some religious teachers in the case of the last one. The messages are conveyed gradually and persistently by the apparatus of an institution that is based on compulsion.

The third tyranny is that of the peer group. Children are compelled to spend 15,000 hours minimum in the forced company of their peers. There is an opportunity cost. They lose the chance to mix with adults out and about in society, and gradually become enrolled and imprisoned in the youth culture instead. The price to be paid varies from an ageist outlook addiction, to clothes-fashion addiction, to pop music addition, to smoking addiction, to drug addiction, to minor and sometimes major crime. Families who decide to opt for home-based education frequently refer to the 'tyranny of the peer group' as one of the key reasons for their decision.

Chris Shute addresses all three tyrannies in turn in his reflections on twenty-five years as a teacher. It is a confessional book, noting how his uneasiness about some of the things he was required to do to children in the name of education grew into a compelling recognition of the nature of compulsory schooling. His observations are drawn from everyday incidents in the lives of the schools he taught in. But more than this, he links those stories with the reflective work of people like Alice Miller, who studied the educational experiences of the members of the Third Reich and how they helped create the monsters of the Nazi regime.

Chris Shute, like John Holt and others, thinks schools could be rescued from their poisonous pedagogy. So do I, but I remain pessimistic. In the race that H G Wells identified between education and catastrophe, the latter seems to be well ahead.

Roland Meighan

Special Professor of Education, University of Nottingham

Preface

I am convinced that undiluted authoritarian schooling, whatever its nominal purpose may be, conditions young people to be unfree. It creates an environment in which people who conform to Authority's arbitrary rules and agree with its views about life and learning get a reward, whilst those who set off down their own paths are punished severely. It confers on book learning and abstract thought a prestige to which they are not necessarily entitled, and it makes children think that if they are not gifted at a wide variety of subjects they are 'stupid', 'not bright', failing life's crucial tests. This state of affairs is completely unacceptable in a society which thinks of itself as 'advanced'.

Respect and freedom

It follows that something must be done, soon and with determination, to change our education system so that it recognises the right of every child to grow up amidst respect and freedom.

Our self-interest as a nation should impel us to want freedom for our children. In this century alone we have fought two great World Wars and an almost uncountable number of small ones to preserve what we think of as essential freedoms. We went against Hitler and the Fascists as if they and their system of political thought came from an alien planet. Yet all fascists and all authoritarians began as babies and went through whatever systems existed in their country to bring them to adulthood, just as our children do.

A disease-causing society

The oppression which people like Hitler visited on the world did not happen because evil spirits got into them, or because they went mad, but because a whole generation of Europeans grew up in a society where only male adults counted for anything, and where obedience and submission were the only virtues which parents recognised in their children. Armoured against compassion by the very fact that they had not themselves experienced it and unable to imagine a community not rigidly controlled by its strongest members, they lost no time in smashing democracy.

Might is wrong

We who claim to value democracy above all other types of government ought to see to it that nothing in our education system teaches children that might is right, or that decisions which affect people need not be based upon those peoples' views of life. At the moment, we have a school system in which nothing important ever happens because its pupils express a need for it and, most culpably of all, obedience, conformity and compliance are valued but a child who follows his or her own programme is punished and made to feel wicked.

Chapter one

Schools are bad places for children

This book is about schools and what they do to their pupils.

It is not a respectful book. I do not share the belief current in most of the civilised world that school is a good place for all children to spend the early part of their lives, and I feel no need to speak as if I did. I think schooling is a waste of many pupils' time, and a cause of lifelong misery for some.

Anyone who thinks that the problem of modern education can be solved simply by spending more money on schools, or by making teachers work 'harder' will be annoyed, even disgusted by my words. Teachers, especially, will react strongly to the implications of what I shall say about the work to which they have dedicated their lives. I apologise to them sincerely. Not because I regret anything I have said, but because I know that many teachers are idealistic people who forgo the chance to make money out of their skill in order to pass it on to the next generation. They do not deserve to be criticised for a failing which is, as I shall try to show, inherent in the very fabric of the schooling system. Unfortunately they are the ones who operate that system and define its human aspects. Therefore I shall have to include them in my general criticism.

I have been a teacher for more than twenty five years. Like many others I came into the profession because I was enthusiastic about learning and believed most other children were too. I saw teaching as a way to turn my own love of books and study to good account.

As I gained more experience of real life in the classroom I discovered that a substantial number of children in school hated being there. This ought to have worried me more than it did. At the time I saw difficult pupils as a minor problem. I assumed that they were 'going through a phase', or suffering from a 'bad home background'. The main thing was to contain them and not allow them to spoil the work of other pupils.

The teachers who seemed to have the most success with the difficult pupils were, of course, the autocratic disciplinarians. Like any young teacher I tended to imitate them. I watched their uncompromising determination to have their own way in the classroom, and I did my best to reproduce it in my classes. I failed as often as I succeeded, but when I did manage to hold down an unruly class I felt I was achieving something valuable. Naturally, when my turn came to supervise student teachers I told them the well-tried, oft-repeated secret of success: 'Hold them down at any cost. You can't teach effectively until you have established your control!'

The space warp

It was a lad called Terry who first made me doubt the value of 'old-fashioned' discipline. He was 15, a stocky East London lad, intelligent enough to get into grammar school but more wily than academic. He and I were more or less permanently at war. I could not control him and he did not like me—or so it seemed as we lurched from crisis to crisis, measuring out our days together with detentions, beatings and endless confrontations.

One morning, as I travelled to school in the tube, steeling myself for yet another round of unpleasantness with Terry, he got into the carriage and sat down beside me. 'Hullo, Sir!', he said pleasantly. 'Hullo, Terry!' I replied, trying to keep out of my voice any disappointment that he had come to disturb my peace before I was mentally ready for it. He started to talk animatedly about his pastimes, his home life and his plans for the future. I waited in vain for him to misbehave.

We talked together most enjoyably until we reached the station where we were to get off. He went with me out of the station, across the main road and down the side street which led to the school. Still he was polite and restrained. Only when we reached the school and went in did he revert to his 'normal' behaviour. It was as if we had stepped through some bizarre space warp into a parallel universe, where I was once again the enemy. He ran off, jeering, to join his mates. I ceased to believe in miracles.

Explosive ideas

This incident made me ask a simple, but, as I came to see, fundamental question about schools as places where we give children what we think of as education. How was it that a person who behaved as if he hated me in school could be so reasonable outside? If, as I suspected, the change in his behaviour was caused by his being in school, how could we, as a society, justify paying me and my colleagues to keep him there? Outside school he was pleasant and mature. In school he was irresponsible and abrasive. It seemed to me even then very much as if he would have been better off somewhere else.

Naturally I could not take that line of thinking much further at the time. After all, I had chosen to devote my life to schooling children. If I concluded that schools were bad places for children I should have no alternative but to go away and do something different. At the time I was neither courageous enough nor blessed with sufficient imagination to think of that, so I carried on and made the best fist I could of being a grammar school teacher.

At the same time, the Penguin Education books introduced me to John Holt. I read *How children fail*, in which Holt suggests, on the basis of his observations in an American elementary school, that children respond to being in school not by embracing every opportunity to learn from the teachers, but rather by trying to find ways of fitting in with what they see as the main purpose of school—to give the teachers right answers so that they will leave you alone and concentrate on someone else. He demonstrated, with examples taken from the behaviour of his own students, how children consistently avoided using the teacher's model of logical thought to answer the questions. Instead they resorted to an elaborate apparatus of ploys to trick the teachers into indicating what 'sort' of answer they were looking for. As a result many children contrived to spend hour after hour 'participating' in lessons, even giving 'correct' responses from time to time, without learning anything.

Worse still, he suspected, as I came to suspect, that the children were losing their natural and acquired abilities to learn, the abilities which enabled each one of them to master his or her native language without formal lessons, simply by living with people and listening to them, imitating them and responding to their encouragement.

I suppose every teacher has a place in his or her mind where ideas are stored about education which are known about because the people who formulated them bear the 'stamp of greatness', but which it would seem to be folly to take out of the lecture hall and into the classroom. I am thinking of Rousseau's 'Emile', or A S Neill's writings about Summerhill. In that place I filed Holt's ideas and my own misgivings. I spent many years trying to do a normal, respectable job of teaching in a variety of schools, without allowing doubt or dissatisfaction to interfere with my work. In the end, however, the dangerous, explosive ideas I had been harbouring broke out and forced me to look at them again.

From academe...

Working in a grammar school insulates one from some of the more abrasive aspects of teaching. The pupils have, generally speaking, expressed some wish to be in the school in the first place. They have passed an examination designed to show their ability to cope with academic work and abstract thought. Their parents have probably impressed upon them how good it is to 'get to the grammar school', and until adolescence begins to impose its own agenda of change and uncertainty, I have always found it fairly easy to teach them.

In a grammar school it is rarely necessary to answer the question 'Why are we doing this work?' Pupils accept with good grace that if you go to a selective school you have to do a certain amount of difficult learning, more or less because it *is* difficult. They may not like the work, but since they want the qualifications and career prospects which it leads to, teaching them is not excessively troublesome. When I was a grammar school teacher, I tried to make my lessons reasonably endurable, but I rarely felt that I needed to win the pupils' attention. By and large the content of the lesson, and my ability to answer questions about it was stimulation enough.

... to the front line

Later I worked in comprehensive schools. It was a chastening experience. No longer could I rely on the pupils' basic motivation to learn my subject, a motivation which had sustained me as a grammar school teacher. Suddenly I was confronted by classes of children who expected to be dominated, controlled and seduced into learning.

Teaching became for me less of an intellectual activity and more like a battle in which I was destined to lose some of my humanity—because I am at bottom a fairly placid person. I would rather negotiate than fight. My more old-fashioned colleagues hastened to point out that negotiating with adolescents in school is usually a waste of time.

I ought to have had the wit to ask why they thought this. After all, weren't we there to teach the children how adults behave? Shouldn't we be ashamed if after nine or ten years under our professional care they still could not be reasoned with and persuaded to co-operate with us? When I was teaching I had other preoccupations, but now I feel that those questions need and deserve an answer. In fact, I think they are so important that until the teaching profession addresses itself to them it will fail, abjectly and indefensibly, in its duty to a substantial number of its clients.

If schooling produces young people many of whom are deeply disaffected, unwilling to listen to reason, and incapable of behaving socially unless dominated by some powerful leader, the time has come to ask whether the schooling system is solving problems or generating them.

Fostering the fascist state of mind

After 25 years of teaching I have come to the conclusion that schools do indeed create in some pupils—possibly most—a state of mind which no honest educator would consciously set out to produce. Worse, I contend that the effect of schooling is to suppress in young people the very traits of character which could be most valuable to them as mature citizens of a modern, complex democracy. Instead it reinforces the mentality which enabled strutting buffoons like Hitler and Mussolini to lead their nations to destruction.

To talk about fascism in the same breath as schools, is, of course, disturbing. School education is a secular religion, a repository for our aspirations to social virtue and improvement. Fascism is a damnable system which cauterised the conscience of countless people to the point where they were capable of killing defenceless people merely because they belonged to a racial group deemed inferior, or held views contrary to those of their killers. It was a political machinery which devoured human beings, having first seduced them and poisoned them with a superficially heroic call to revolutionary ardour.

The very idea that there could be some organic relationship between schools and fascism challenges our sensibility in a unique way. If there were any truth at all in it the education service, which is full of decent people who loathe oppression, would be morally bound to reform its structure and its purposes from the root.

I intend to show in this book that schooling is, indeed, an activity which has aspects in common with fascism. That is not to say that teachers mean it to be so, or that they are conscious of the evil in which they are involved. Even fascism in its early phases attracted some reasonable, high-minded people who believed that the world could be changed for the better merely by the use of a little force and rigour in the right place.

The tragedy of this century is that so many of those ordinary, reasonable folk identified themselves so completely with the fascist way that they could not discern the point in its development when its essential malignancy began to appear. To the extent that teachers are unable, or unwilling to see the oppression and the pain some pupils experience in school I have to say that to me they are part of the same tragedy, and no less worthy of blame.

Chapter two

Fascism as a tendency

Fascism to me is a graphic word which describes an attitude towards people. It reached its lowest point of unspeakable vileness in the concentration camps of Nazi Germany, but it was coined at the beginning of the century by people who were casting around for nothing more evil than a way to organise society.

Government by contempt

It seemed to such people that liberalism and democracy, whatever might be said in their favour, did not work. Ordinary people, they thought, were too stupid, too sentimental for their own good. If left to run their own affairs they soon fell into chaos or poverty. Government could only be successful if it were in the hands of hard determined men. They, and no-one else, could be trusted to take tough decisions. Those decisions might be cruel, even barbaric, but if they brought glory to the nation they were amply justified.

Such ideas needed a potent symbol. The Italians found it in the 'fasces'. This was an axe bound up with a bundle of rods and carried in procession before public officials in ancient Rome. It stood for their authority, particularly their right to have wrongdoers beaten and executed. When the fascists took it as the sign of their movement, they forgot that the Romans, hard though they were, respected law. The people whom they punished had been judged. We would probably call that judgement harsh. Nonetheless, there was nothing arbitrary about it. To suffer under Roman law you had to have done something illegal. Under the fascist regimes you could suffer unspeakable punishment simply for being who you were, holding unauthorised opinions, or just for being in the wrong place at the wrong time.

Whatever its founders thought they were starting, fascism as it developed became a system of ideas which could be crudely summed up like this:

■ Society is, and must always be, stratified.

■ In the nature of things, the majority—who are ignorant, weak and collectively worth very little—must be ruled by the few who are enlightened.

■ The rulers may—indeed they must—do whatever is needed to make the ruled obey them. Only in this way can society achieve the aims which the rulers have decided upon.

■ If the ruled do not like this scheme of things and show signs of rebellion they must be crushed.

■ Every aspect of society must be controlled by the rulers in order that it might contribute to achieving their goals. This might well mean changing the way people use langu͏   ͏that words come to mean what the rulers want them to mean.

■ Good rulers become mo͏   ͏ defined as those who allow no human ͏   ͏ them aside from their purpo͏

A well-meaning tyranny

I want to suggest that this programme closely rese͏   ͏ average school. In place of 'rulers' and 'ruled' put 'teachers and ͏   ͏ you have the hidden agenda of many secondary schools today.

It isn't what people intend, of course. Schools are full of good adults with impeccable human qualities who genuinely believe in the value of what they are doing. My quarrel is not with what they believe. I am only concerned with what actually happens. I want to talk about the real results of schooling. More particularly, I want to discuss schooling as it affects the 'difficult' pupil, the child who for any of a score of reasons cannot or does not wish to be a docile citizen of the school-state.

Since the beginning of civilisation, children have posed a problem to adults. Their smallness, their incompleteness when compared with adults, makes them inconvenient to have around. True, their parents may well love them, and other adults may tend to feel sentimentally patronising towards them or to see them as cute, that is, endearingly naive. Yet this is an adult world. It works the way adults want it to. Not to be an adult can easily make a false note in the symphony everyone is supposed to be playing.

Children disturb adults in a number of potent ways. They are naturally egotistical (as many adults are) but they have not yet learned to feel guilty about it. They do not know—and even when they do know they do not understand—the game of token self-denial so familiar to adults. Their egotism is, unlike that of older people, innocent. They simply do not yet know enough about other peoples' feelings to sympathise with them.

Children are also indiscreet. Their feelings come to the surface quickly and often dramatically. They do not understand that you have to hold back your tears, your laughter and your curiosity until you can express them without embarrassing others, which may be never, or not until you have forgotten what the fuss was about.

Adults react to being disturbed by trying to remove the source of the disturbance. This is unfortunate for many children because the adults who control them remember how their parents treated them when they were young. They forget how much pain and confusion they themselves suffered from 'traditional' English parental discipline, but it gives them a clear idea of the steps they have to take to bring their own children under control. So the cycle of telling-off, punishment and repression goes on. It is immensely difficult to break into it because it seems natural and 'sensible' to treat children as if they were a mixture of plaything, petty criminal and mental patient.

Progress...

Our picture of children is more complex than that, of course. Many children live happily with their parents most of the time, and many parents feel confident enough to reason and negotiate with their youngsters rather than punishing them. In recent years the public has begun to see how easily adults can misuse their power over children. A healthy concern has grown up for the safety of youngsters, who used to suffer cruelty and abuse because of the tradition which held that you must never listen to children or believe what they say. Yet in our schools the old patterns still prevail.

... and its enemies

A school, like a fascist state, is about the business of compelling people to conform to a pattern of behaviour and a way of thinking decided by the few who hold power over them. The adults who run it have been trained to assume that they 'know best' and that their pupils are in the school in order to receive a kind of mental 'adjustment' which only they can give them. As a result, every aspect of the children's behaviour which gives expression to their newness on Earth, their incompleteness, the fact that they are not grown-up strengthens the teachers' belief that their work is necessary and valuable to their pupils.

That belief, reinforced as it is by the notion that schooling 'works' even when the pupils resist it, becomes the catch-all justification for a set-up which, I contend, deserves to be denounced because it distorts, oppresses and violates the natural integrity of young, vulnerable minds.

In the simplest possible terms, then, schools are fascistic when they treat children not as if they were immensely complex, unique organisms, precious and vulnerable, but rather as if they were wayward underlings needing restraint and firm training.

If you believe that children, by their nature, need to be dealt with as helpless inferiors it does not make you a fascist in the full, committed sense of the term. It does not mean that you are necessarily capable of the cruelty and the utter contempt for civilised values for which political fascism was, and is, notorious. However, I want to suggest, as courteously as I can, that you may share, unwittingly, values in common with those of the fascists.

No-one seriously involved with schooling sets out to harm children. Yet children emerge from the system harmed. Fascism is not dead: our schools still produce children who go into adult life expecting to be controlled, and falling gratefully into the clutches of any demagogue who can convince them that he or she will stand no nonsense from them.

We owe it to all of our young to see that they learn thoroughly the lessons of history. Therefore it is our duty to ensure that they leave our schools armed with a clear understanding of how freedom can die in a nation. And above all, it is our responsibility to treat them when they are young in a way which strengthens their delight in being themselves and their respect for others.

Chapter three

School—an environment for fascism

Bruno Bettleheim, the psychologist and educator, spent time in Dachau concentration camp. While he was there he studied the strategies which the inmates used to survive their unspeakable experience. He came to the conclusion that the prisoners who were most successful in keeping the core of their being intact under almost unimaginable pressure were those who adapted their behaviour so that it corresponded with the character which the guards attributed to them.

The guards. thought of them as subhuman, stupid and worthless because they were Jews. They saved their lives by behaving as if they accepted their sub-humanity and stupidity. Bettleheim saw university lecturers, doctors, lawyers and academics smiling vacantly, tripping over their own feet, misunderstanding orders and talking like children. Their pantomime reassured the guards and protected the prisoners from a certain proportion of the cruelty which happened to inmates who had not yet learned the unwritten rules of camp life.

From his experience Bettleheim created a therapy based on the assumption that people with emotional traumas respond not only to speech but also to the environment created for them by the therapist. Having himself lived in a place which tended to infantilise people and destroy their ability to behave like free adults, he saw that emotional strength and true self-confidence could only grow where it was utterly safe to be an individual, and where freedom was valued and pursued seriously. Therefore he strove to eliminate from his patients' surroundings anything which might abridge their freedom to be serious, sensitive, human beings.

In his school for difficult children Bettleheim established a regime which was radical and therapeutic. He was able, with the help of mature and dedicated educators, to take severely damaged children and rehabilitate them. It is not my purpose here to talk a great deal about this methods, except to mention his way of dealing with children who ran away from school.

The right to run away

The school would send an educator to find the absconding child, but the adult would never try to drag the youngster back as if he or she had done something wrong. Instead, the educator would do his or her best to go where the child went, following quietly but persistently, until the fugue was over.

By all accounts the method worked. At least it acknowledged that you cannot change the mind of an angry, desperate young person with compulsion, because even a warm, kindly environment may be wrong for him or her at a particular time and there needs to be the right to get away from it. If the school had compelled an absconding youngster to return by force it would have transformed itself into a mild form of concentration camp. All its therapeutic work would have gone for nothing.

I have noticed in my own classes children behaving like the Dachau prisoners whom Bettleheim observed. Like him, I have seen the stupid smile, the exaggerated clumsiness and displays of hypocritical obsequiousness. I suspect that children display these behaviours because they are unfree, locked into surroundings which irritate them and stifle their personalities.

The warp revisited

As a teacher, particularly towards the end of my career, as I came to be more aware of the issues I am discussing here, I noticed that the children I was supposed to be educating were responding to their environment. The boy I mentioned in my introduction, who behaved badly in school but was perfectly reasonable outside, displayed a reaction which I have seen many times since in every type of school. I have often seen children change their behaviour in a moment as they moved from one part of the school to another. I even learned to predict how the shape and dimensions of a corridor or classroom would affect them.

I noticed, for instance, that children became noisier in large, echoing places, particularly wide corridors. They seemed to feel that the very length and openness of them was an incitement to run and shout. Since running and shouting are at one and the same time natural things for children to do, in season and out of season, and extremely annoying to adults, I suspect that school architecture has contributed to a fair amount of conflict between young and old over the years!

Dark satanic mills?

The environment which is school is, of course, more than just a function of its architecture. But the physical shape of a school is a powerful influence in the moulding of its internal dynamic. An old-fashioned board school—of which there are still many—tells everyone who uses it a great deal about what its original builders saw as the purpose of education. The resemblance of such a school to a mill, factory, a barracks or a ship of the line, is by no means accidental. It was built to impress upon children that the society in which they were to live had no room in it for the folk who refused to stand in line, march from place to place and fit into the machinery whose productivity they were there to enhance.

We no longer build schools like that, but we still use them, and even in our newer school buildings we have not broken away radically from the fundamental picture of the school as a model of the controlled, directed life which we want the children to think they are going to live when they grow up. We still make our young spend their formative years in angular boxes linked by corridors, full of places where it is an offence to run, shout, play noisy games or do anything spontaneous.

The school, then, is an environment dedicated to fostering in the young people who live in it, a specific array of ideas about the purpose of life and their part in it. I believe that those ideas are tainted. More specifically, I think they are fascist.

Lines of power

Anyone who has seen Leni Riefenstahl's 1930's film of the Nuremburg rally in Nazi Germany will have thought hard about what happens when people are gathered together, dressed in uniform and made to stand in rows listening to an orator. The lines of stormtroopers, each one encased in the anonymity of a field-grey battledress, broad rimmed helmet and identical equipment, suggest not people preparing to co-operate in some worthwhile human endeavour, but rather machinery waiting to be used.

Perhaps there were decent people in the ranks who were already questioning the Nazi ideals of conscienceless power and unyielding will, but once locked into the living machine of the rally, their moral autonomy yielded to the flow of power from the demagogue on the main dais. The symbolic regularity and rigidity of their formation denatured them and impressed upon them both their insignificance as individuals and the omnipotence of the movement whose leader was Adolf Hitler.

Cultivating democracy

I hope that serious educators in contemporary Europe set a unique value upon democracy. Those who remember the Second World War and the years which followed it, the spread of Stalin's tyranny even as Hitler's collapsed, will surely have realised that free, popular and moderate government does not flourish naturally. It has to be guarded and nurtured. When it produces vacillation and uncertainty as it struggles to reconcile various interests within the nation, we have to protect it against the power-merchants who would rather tidy things up with a strong dose of tyranny. And above all we must establish in the mind of every citizen the principle that government is, as far as humanly possible, intended to benefit people and enable them to spend their lives happily.

Therefore I contend that if education in a democratic society is to help that society to survive, it must encourage young people to value their own specialness and respect the specialness of others. It must give every child opportunities to find out what it is that he or she, uniquely, can do, without harming anyone else. It must at all costs respectfully allow each child to discover a role in the cosmic drama of humanity. If it fails, democracy and all that goes with it may be trampled again.

Growth or decay?

Does the general ethos of our schools, particularly our secondary schools, tend to favour the growth of strong democratic feelings in our children? Or does it convey to them, both directly and by the subtle influence of the symbols which help to define it, the message that they are not in school to take initiatives or to use their creative powers, and that they must do what the school says is good for them to do—or risk a heavy regime of punishment and deprivation?

When I started teaching, my older colleagues impressed on me that children 'need' a framework of order. For instance, it was important to see that they lined up outside classrooms and in other places where they were gathered together, like the hall before assembly and the playground at the end of breaktime. In the classroom itself it was important that I, as the teacher, should decide where they sat, and that their friends should not be together if it meant that they would be tempted to talk when they should be listening to me.

I accepted all this in the way any beginner in a profession accepts the word of more experienced colleagues. It did not occur to me at the time to ask how the children felt about it. Later, however, I saw chilling parallels with fascist rallies. I realised that lining people up is a potent preliminary to manipulating them. If a group of individuals have, effectively, only one formation in which they can stand and one direction in which they are permitted to move, their capacity to think narrows—in the moral domain as much as the intellectual—to the point where the one who commands the gathering controls them whether he or she deserves to or not.

Does teacher know best?

I imagine that most teachers think that they are well qualified to tell children what to do. Perhaps they are, though I have met a few in my time whom I should be reluctant to let within hailing distance of vulnerable youngsters. But to confer the right to manipulate and coerce children on a class of people whose raison d'etre is nominally little more than that they know about French, science or whatever, is surely dangerous.

It is dangerous not only because it saps the youngsters' ability to think and act for themselves, but also because in the long run, unless they find the courage to question the regime under which they live—usually a perilous thing to do—they risk becoming used to obedience. It is generally right to accept the reasonable rules of a properly regulated society. I have no objection to that. But if people grow up expecting to be controlled and made to obey, and if they come to believe that the sort of person who can wield power over them is morally superior to the one who cannot, or does not wish to, the journey to Nuremburg and Dachau need not be a long one for the nation to which those people belong.

The culture of hardness

Far from being alien to our concept of schooling, the culture of hardness—the bias to violence as a way of settling differences which marks the history of most European nations in the early part of this century—is inseparable from it.

We send children to school knowing that up to a quarter of them will be bullied at some time. Instead of demanding that the school treat this oppression as a serious problem some teachers trivialise it and insist that the victims cause their own plight by not 'standing up for themselves'. Parents sometimes reinforce this idea by telling the boy or girl who has been bullied to give the bully a dose of his or her own medicine instead of complaining to adults. In this way, from their earliest years, many children come to believe that it is 'right' to suppress any feelings of pity and concern for other children which they may have, in order to be strong and socially dominant.

I have often had to deal with the problems of quiet, gentle children who had become unpopular with the rest of the class. Sometimes they were youngsters whose religious or moral convictions forbade them to join in the rough and tumble of school life. Sometimes they were children with a quirky, difficult character which would, perhaps, have made life unhappy for them in any group. I found it hard to change the attitude of the other children towards them. There was in almost every situation an undercurrent of feeling, shared by both pupils and teachers, that it was the victim's fault that he or she was bullied. It was almost as if the victim was oppressing the bully by putting irresistible temptation in peoples' way!

Of course, in the end the system stirred itself, sided with the victim, and punished the bully. But until recently it was most unusual for anybody involved with education to suggest that all children should be protected, systematically and continuously, from classroom oppression. In the past two or three years, since a plethora of scandals involving the bullying and abuse of children drove us to start listening to them seriously, we have begun to care more about their emotional well-being. Courses have been created for schools which make children look at bullying from the victim's point of view. Some schools have even set up 'bully courts' to bring bullies to account.

Why has it taken so long?

All this is good, though still not widespread. The problem our schools face is that, for all their good intentions, it has taken more than a hundred years for anyone involved with them to start a campaign against bullying. Something in their atmosphere seems to disable the normal instincts of the intelligent, professional adults who work in them, so that moral priorities which to an outsider seem essential become almost marginal compared with questions of authority, uniformity and academic success.

Teachers are corrupted too

Children are not the only ones whose behaviour is distorted by being in school. Teachers also find their personalities jarred and corrupted by the work they have to do.

Controlling children and making them perform mental tricks is an unnatural skill which does not necessarily go with having knowledge and wanting to share it. Unfortunately, teachers have discovered by bitter experience that if they cannot play the class control game it matters little how much knowledge they have. They have to teach captive audiences of children, many of whom have expressed no interest in the lessons they are trying to give. Therefore teaching them has to begin with an assault on the indifference or hostility of some pupils to the very idea of being in the class in the first place.

Our present picture of school makes the average teacher behave like a sort of doctor whose patients are all suffering from a disease called ignorance. If the pupils happen to be bright, interested youngsters who accept the teaching, the 'treatment' will be easy and pleasant for all concerned. If, on the other hand, the class has elements in it who see no need for learning the lesson, the teacher will have to find some way to restrain their energy and wrench their attention away from whatever thoughts and interests they have brought with them to the lesson. Unless the teacher has some charisma, or the ability to entertain children, this is likely to be the hardest and most worrying aspect of the teaching. How he or she tackles it may decide whether a happy, successful career is the result, or thirty years in an ante-room of Hell to look forward to.

Since so much hangs upon control, teachers work immensely hard at it, and sometimes use methods which appall more scrupulous people outside the profession. I have read more than once in the newspapers, reports of teachers who have tried to control children by taping their mouths or tying them to their chairs. Methods like these are generally the last resort of a teacher in despair, who may be dismissed for using them, but in my experience the more acceptable ways of suppressing the children's resistance are not necessarily more humane.

A special message

I remember an experience which vividly illustrates the way in which schools turn normal teachers into people who are, though they do not realise it, no longer educators, but something else. I was teaching French to some children who did not want to learn it. I had controlled them, but only just, and the atmosphere in the room was tense.

The bell went for the end of the lesson and the children boiled out into the hall, whooping and hollering like freed slaves. Then a small group of boys came to see me. I thought they were going to be insolent in some way, to see if my bite was as bad as my bark. Instead, one of them said, quietly: 'We hate X. He loves hurting people.' Just that. Then they went quietly off to lunch, leaving me holding their bundle of resentment against one of my colleagues.

I was bewildered because I sensed that I had been given a very important and serious message, but I could think of no reason why I should have been chosen to receive it. In any case, there was nothing I could do about it, because X counted for a great deal more in the school's power structure than I did. On the other hand, I felt that I had been entrusted with a human responsibility, a communication distinctive because of its honesty, sent out in the hope that somehow it might change things.

The classrom gladiators

I tell the story here partly to discharge the obligation I feel that boy laid on me. I hasten to add that X, whom I know quite well, was not an especially cruel or unfeeling person. Some of his methods were admirably modern and even child-centred, and he produced some enviable results. However, he also practised a form of class control which was firmly based on 'old-fashioned' attitudes to children. He tended to focus his dominance by putting children down more or less continuously with heavy handed sarcasm. He would probably have agreed that he hurt the children's feelings from time to time, but he would have insisted that they deserved it. In any case, as he once observed to me: 'Either I win or they do—and there's no way they are going to win!'

I have met many teachers like him. They are the natural creation of a school system which has not yet understood how insidiously bad education can displace good simply because it is easier to practise and gives greater satisfaction to adults. That it also crushes many pupils and embitters them, that it contributes materially to the petty banditry and asocial behaviour of many older children means nothing to classroom gladiators like X. The cause is far enough removed from the effect to allow a complacent teaching profession to treat them as if they were not related. And no-one has yet had the wit to find a valid test by which to assess the life-long effect of schooling on pupils, so teachers will never have to ask themselves whether they are helping to improve the attitudes which are abroad in society, or to make them worse.

In simple terms

In simple terms, then, schools tend to harm their pupils by putting them in an environment where they need to set aside important areas of their natural constitution in order to survive. School discourages children from maturing socially by surrounding them with evidence that they are powerless and ignorant, and by enforcing on them a code of petty restrictions. These often have no value beyond the control which they enable teachers and other adults to exert over youngsters. Generally they have no moral content whatever.

School is also a place where adults can inflict a wide spectrum of cruelties on children without having to recognise what they are doing or shoulder any responsibility for it. I accept that there are pupils and teachers who are happy with their experience of school. However, my concern is with the undoubted fact that all the dangers I have mentioned can exist in a school, unrecognised by anyone, since adults are blind to them and children, even if they dimly perceive the wrong which is being done to them, know full well that nothing they can say, no protest that they make, will ever be listened to.

Chapter four

The question of justice

People who suffer injustice when they are young tend to behave unjustly when they are older. I should have thought that was simple common sense. Unfortunately, in spite of all our talk about human rights, we do not guarantee justice to our schoolchildren.

Few adults, I imagine, find themselves in trouble with the law more than once or twice in a lifetime, probably for nothing more serious than exceeding the speed limit. They tend to assume that if by some awful mischance they were charged with an offence which they had not committed, the basic good sense behind our legal system would protect them and see to it that they were found not guilty.

This conveniently uncritical approach to justice can operate in a moderately democratic society without producing too many *causes célèbres*, because the traditions which form our national spirit are powerful enough to have created in most British people a real revulsion against flagrant injustice. We are still, even after a spate of quashed sentences including the Birmingham Six in 1991 and the Guildford Four in 1992, a nation which expects fair play from its police.

Different standards

In schools, however, different standards apply. When I started teaching, in a tough part of London, I learned that if you wanted to control the children successfully you had to behave as if the reality of what was happening in the classroom was under your control, and no-one else's. Simply, you had to convince the pupils that you knew what was going on and that you would stamp heavily on anyone whose behaviour you did not like. Once you had persuaded them that you, and you alone, decided what was right or wrong in your lessons, the children became docile and manageable. Since any sound or motion of theirs could get them into trouble if you chose to treat it as an offence, the safest thing for them to do was—nothing.

T's war

At the time I had no difficulty with that idea. I visited a lesson given by my Head of Department, who believed very strongly in uncompromising control. What I saw there impressed me so much that for a long time afterwards, in spite of some misgivings, I struggled to imitate him.

T, the Head of Department, was near the end of his career. He had been teaching all his adult life, and, as he told me often, no pupil had ever challenged him. As we went into the room the children's conversation, already subdued, was turned off like a tap at the main.

The lesson which followed was archetypal—orderly, clear, totally controlled and innocent of any child-centredness or free activity. As I look back on it I am struck by the ironical fact that T, an old-fashioned Communist, gave the kind of lesson which would have delighted the most right-wing Tory education minister. The children were frozen to their desks, as utterly compliant as it was possible for adolescents to be.

Yet T behaved as if they were on the verge of rebellion. The sheer aggressiveness with which he spoke to them, his insistence on being called 'Monsieur' when they answered his questions and the way in which he rebuked them for interruptions too quiet for me to hear, made him look as if he were taming lions, not educating children.

The only way?

At the end of the lesson my admiration for the man's control was already at war with a nagging sense that for all his certainty and determination he was doing something which my instincts told me was foreign to education. I could not see clearly then what it was, because I shared with him the idea that children 'needed' to be held down. They lacked self-control and maturity, and it was for self-controlled, mature people like me to govern them firmly until they became adults. Nonetheless, I realised even then that those children were suffering.

Crime and punishment

It was as if they had committed a crime, for which the punishment was to sit in complete silence doing exactly as they were told. No child, I imagine, would have chosen to undergo that lesson if there had been any alternative open. From the tension in the classroom I gauge that some of the children were, if not terrified, at least thoroughly uneasy. If education is a fruitful engagement between the mind of the teacher and that of the taught, then precious little of it happened that day. Rather, the lesson was a reminder to the pupils that in the world of the school they were a subject people, and that as far as T was concerned they could never be subject enough.

Years later, when I had freed myself from the thraldom of that school and its attitudes towards 'discipline' I began to ask myself what effect being schooled under such conditions would have upon the children. Would they look back on it with pleasure and recognise the rigours of T's French classes as a worthwhile experience? It became clear to me that if they did so they would also have to agree with T's assessment of their character and his attitude to their human rights. They would have to accept that 14-year olds naturally deserve to be kept in fear, and constantly rebuked. Any independence of mind, any disposition they might have had to see things differently from their teacher, and above all any hope that they might have nurtured of defending themselves if they disagreed with him, would have to be put aside. Justice for them would be whatever T said it was.

Plus ça change...

The teaching profession in the 1990's possibly thinks that it has grown out of T's approach to pedagogy. I have worked in a number of schools in my time and in each one of them I have been told by the head or other teachers, that 'we have a nice easy relationship with our kids'. Yet in almost every one of them, at least some of the teachers lived by a version of T's code, and their influence was great in the school.

The result, I contend, is that for many children school is an environment in which they experience feelings more calculated to inure them to slavery than to the life of a free citizen. It is a place where they are always in the wrong, unless they are doing exactly what they have been told. In school there is no way a child can complain that a teacher is mishandling him or her, or that the teacher has misunderstood the situation. The internal economy of the school can only work if it is understood by everybody that adults are never wrong and pupils never in the right.

If that sounds unfair—and there are, I am sure, schools where it would be— I can only say that I have seen extreme injustice dealt out regularly to children of all ages in school. I don't mean a few occasional mistakes such as happen in every community, but a systematic denial of essential human rights. I do not suggest that teachers intend this to happen, only that in fact it does. It happens because, in the long run, the school cannot function in any other way.

School is a place where children are made to do things. From their first day in the classroom to moment when they put the whole episode behind them and go into the world as young adults, the school decides, at first gently, then more insistently, how they shall spend their time. Such choices as they are allowed to make are firmly controlled. The teachers may even go as far as to determine what the pupils shall wear, how long their hair must be, and how they shall do their writing.

Almost without exception we have come to regard this state of affairs as normal. We see no need to justify it, or to examine sympathetically cases in which it fails to deliver good education. Yet our schools are full of youngsters who respond to this compulsion with resistance.

Whether they are openly disruptive or simply unwilling to take a full part in lessons and homework the school treats them as enemies. It defines them as an underclass, and metes out to them a generalised oppression made up of tellings-off, detentions, low marks, extra 'remedial' or punitive work and sometimes having to carry a special document which has to be signed after lessons by the teacher.

There's a real person inside that child!

It is worth recalling at this point that I am not trying to describe what the school intends, but what it actually achieves. I have found that when I talk to teachers or parents about the reasons why children fail at school, I hear about curriculum, facilities, methods. and whatever happen to be their prejudices about the system, but never—in more than ten years of active critical discussion—have I met a person who recognised that children have their own, separate, complicated feelings about the school. Almost every adult I speak to seems to be astonished when I suggest that children may be distressed, or even enraged by being told off, or treated in some way which the adults themselves would find intolerable.

'Show me your pass!' 'Ja baas...'

A while ago I was fostering a fifteen-year old boy. He began to take time off from school, and I went to see one of the deputy heads about him. We had a very long talk, and at one point the teacher became very annoyed with me. We were discussing a rule of the school which struck me as thoroughly misconceived. Every pupil was issued with a printed notebook (my lad had lost his) which he or she had to carry around the school. At any time a teacher could demand to see this book. If the teacher had anything to write about the pupil by way of praise or blame, it could be put in the book. The idea was that the parent could read what had been written and somehow 'reinforce' it at home.

I pointed out that the only other people in the world who had to carry pocket-books around with them and show them to authority on demand were non-white South Africans. I suggested that perhaps the children, or some of them, felt demeaned by this business for the same reasons as Black South Africans, forced to show their Pass or have it signed by a white, experience shame and anger hot enough to turn peaceful people into guerrillas.

The teacher was, as I said, very angry. The thought had not occurred to him. In fact he was angry that anyone else should entertain it because to him it was absurd. The school had introduced the system of contact-books to improve communication with parents. There was a worthwhile aim as far as he was concerned, and any feelings the children might have about it had no importance whatever. As a teacher he knew what was best for children, and if they didn't like what he did, it was just too bad.

I went on argue that the truth was exactly contrary to what he thought. After all, I insisted, the pupils' education, when all the expensive teaching and testing is over, is nothing more than what sticks in their heads. If you teach a lesson on Pythagoras' Theorem and the boy or girl sits in the classroom thinking 'I am bored, I am hungry, I do not understand this stuff and I want to go to the loo,' your lesson is not about Pythagoras at all. It's about boredom, hunger, confusion and a full bladder. In the same way, if you give him or her a contact-book to carry around so that you can have a wonderful dialogue with the parents and he or she hates it because it is a reminder that they are still under age and they have no right to a will of their own, the educational effect of your scheme is absolutely nil.

I suppose that if I had been in that teacher's shoes I should have been angry too, because it is certain that the school had no intention to treat its pupils like an underclass. The contact-book just seemed like a good idea. The senior staff who dreamed it up probably thought it would do something for the image of the school as a place where the pupils were rigorously supervised. Anyway, they probably thought, the right sort of pupil would benefit from the ease with which the teachers could write little compliments in the books. The other kind of pupil, naturally, would have to put up with even more criticism and browbeating, but that was what they deserved, and what they had always received in the past, so that was all right too. The terrible truth is, schools cannot see the harm they do, because the very fact that they are schools absolves them from thinking about it.

A glimmer of hope—the end of corporal punishment.

Slowly, things are beginning to change, especially in the matter of corporal punishment. I remember as a boy of nine or ten living in constant fear of being caned. In my primary school, if you were caught doing something the headteacher disapproved of you could be lashed with a stick, and no explanation or mitigating fact could save you.

Geographical injustice

One day in the playground some boys misbehaved near me, and the playground helper, including me in the general razzia, took me to the head. I had never been so frightened or angry in my life. I tried to explain that the other boys were nothing to do with me, that my relationship with them was geographical and nothing more. The head was used to pleas from the scaffold and probably saw them as evidence of poor moral fibre. He beat me anyway, and I imagine he thought no more of the matter after I had left the room.

I remember to this day the pain and the bitter, incendiary rage I felt. If I could have killed him and blasted his infernal school to the four winds I should have done so with a clear conscience. He did not know, as he should have done, indeed as any adult who has responsibility for young people should know, that everything you do to a child you do to a grown man or woman. He thought he was beating a small boy who would soon forget. He was wrong. I am proud to be doing my part towards bringing down the system he stood for.

The 'professionals'

We no longer beat children in state schools. For this small measure of mercy I am as ready as anyone to commend our leaders and lawmakers. Unfortunately the praise which is due to them has to be balanced by the fact that corporal punishment was abolished against the protests of the teaching profession. My own union, the National Association of Schoolmasters and Union of Women Teachers, shamefully claimed for its members the right to beat children if their 'professional judgement' led them to think the children 'deserved' it. I can think of decisions which might benefit from being taken by a trained teacher rather than a lay person, but the cold-blooded determination to inflict pain on the weak, immature body of another human being is not one of them.

I find it deeply disturbing to think that thousands of intelligent people disagree with me about this question of corporal punishment. Good friends of mine, admirable folk who love children and seem to get on well with their own, still insist that civilised life cannot continue if adults are not allowed to hit their youngsters. Behind all their kindness and decency it seems as if the old brutal spirit of the savage past lingers, waiting for its next opportunity to spring out and show us all what it can do.

The problem is that control and authority have become their own justification. You may preach liberalism and child-centredness in education outside school, but you must not ever risk allowing the child to disagree with you in the classroom. In the end, authority and the adult world must emerge victorious.

How can we change things?

How can we change things? How can we give children their rights in an authoritarian establishment like a school?

I do not think we can as long as school is compulsory and governed by the nonsense of a National Curriculum and an absolutely inflexible leaving date. These elements make it so fundamentally unsuited to the education of real human beings, who are diverse in their interests and mature at different rates, that it cannot alter itself enough to meet their needs without falling to pieces.

Before we can turn school into a truly just and benign place for children, we must strip from it the things which make it convenient for adults to work in. For instance, we must, urgently, abolish compulsory attendance. As long as children have to attend school whether they want to or not, teachers will be protected from any knowledge of how they really affect children, and they will be able to maintain the fiction that their pupils always benefit from their lessons, even when everything they do testifies to the contrary.

A different moral universe

We must also look very closely and critically at the moral universe which we create in the school. I have noticed, and it has worried me for many years, that when children come into the school they enter a world in which a new, more rigorous but far less rational system of morality applies. Outside school, 'right' and 'wrong' mean something which any ordinary person, whatever their age, can understand and recognise in their environment. Hitting people, stealing from them, hurting and insulting them, are all clearly wrong. Giving kindness and gentleness are equally clearly right. In school, however, the code is amplified and distorted.

Suddenly the kinds of action the child is expected to recognise as wrong include not wearing certain clothing, or coming to school with shoes that are not of the permitted colour or shape, eating food in certain places at special times, not doing written exercises which have been set, talking (much of the time), running, asking to go to the toilet outside set times, going home when you want to and not coming to lessons which bore or frighten you.

None of these is wrong in itself. There is nothing immoral about not doing homework or missing a lesson. Such actions are inconvenient or worrying to adults, but they are not even remotely 'wrong', and they should not be treated as if they were. School rules should describe the measures which the school community takes to protect its members from each other's thoughtlessness or petty cruelty. To use them for any other purpose is anti-educational.

Who shall make the laws?

Equally anti-educational is the idea that children cannot be trusted to create and administer their own system of laws. The pupils of A S Neill's Summerhill school have been doing that since the 1920's, and in the process have learned a truth which most other people never discover—that good law-making is a tricky business because everyone in the community has a slightly different point of view. Therefore whoever draws up the code of rules for that community must listen to all those who think it might put them at a disadvantage. He or she must change the code so that it does as little damage as possible to their interests. Only then can the community reasonably call on all its members to obey the rules or suffer some kind of penalty.

In a school, however, the rules by which the children live are almost always drawn up behind closed doors by the Head and the staff—or even by the Head alone. No wonder that the children have little respect for them. There is absolutely no reason why they should, unless we assume that there is some virtue in unthinking obedience to laws laid down by unelected despots. The laws of Britain are legitimate and binding on us all because we elected the people who passed them, and we can throw them out and choose different legislators if we want to. If that is the model of government we want to commend to our children we ought to see that their school rules are drawn up in the same way.

Some readers may scoff at this. I have rarely met an adult who coped easily with the idea of children making rules, because they so often break the ones the adults make for them. Indeed, even in those rare schools where the children help decide community laws we can be sure that there are many youngsters who do not obey the rules all the time. Yet I am convinced that it is better for rules to be made by those who have to obey them, because at the very least the community can then say to those who do not obey: 'Look, you helped to make these laws, you had a chance to discuss them and say what you thought of them. Now, do the decent thing and obey them, for they are your laws as much as they are ours.'

The most worthwhile result of giving children the right to make their own laws would be that teachers would no longer have to act alone as the school's police force.

Chapter five

A totalitarian curriculum

Hand over your minds!

The school curriculum is either nourishment or poison. It cannot be neutral. I believe it is poison.

The time children spend in formal classroom learning is time during which they can do nothing else, even if they want to very much and their minds are poised to absorb some exciting idea which lies outside the curriculum. The teacher, the confining walls of the classroom, the equipment on the desks before them all focus their attention inexorably on the intellectual activity which has been chosen for them to do. As long as the lesson lasts the pupils must hand over their minds to the teacher and the lesson, and accept that he or she will be entitled to punish them for anything they do that breaks the flow of the teaching.

There is no room in this scheme of things for spontaneity or even for curiosity. I am sure many teachers believe that they encourage their pupils to ask questions and exercise their minds independently, and I should be happy to accept that many of them do, from time to time, succeed in this. Nonetheless, I cannot accept that the way we run our schools actually favours lively questioning or the pursuit of ideas which interest the children.

Dangerous questions

Imagine, if you will, what would happen to an ordinary teacher who allowed the pupils freely to ask questions at any point in a lesson. I do not mean just questions about the work in hand, but rather about anything which happened to be going on in their minds. He or she would find that they were answering all sorts of inquiries, some serious, some disobliging or frivolous, yet others showing very clearly that a proportion of their charges were not even really in the room with them, but rather wandering mentally through the enthralling landscapes of childhood. If teachers tried to answer them they could not avoid putting the formal lesson aside for as long as it took to satisfy the children's curiosity, not to mention their desire to avoid being taught.

It would not be long before the teacher felt a growing unease. However stimulating his or her question-and-answer session might seem to be, the system would remind them imperiously that they were not being paid to encourage free-ranging enquiry but to teach the National Curriculum.

Every day teachers face the moral conflict implicit in their contract of work. They must choose between responding to their children's real interests and getting through the curriculum. In a state school there can be no contest. The curriculum wins every time, as it has been doing since formal schooling began. As a result countless children undergo the same teaching. If they enjoy it because it meets their needs and equips them efficiently with the exact knowledge the adult world expects them to have, well and good. This probably happens in some cases, but certainly not all.

Worthwhile knowledge

For the children whose interests lie well outside the National Curriculum, being in school is little more than a prolonged, systematic violation of their minds. The National Curriculum assumes that some knowledge is so worthwhile that no-one may be allowed to avoid learning it. By defining that knowledge in detail and imposing it upon all schools except those in the private sector, the Curriculum effectively divides the nation's children into two communities: the ones who at school age enjoy academic book-learning, and the ones who do not. The latter group, confused by ideas which have no resonance in their minds, pre-occupied with interests for which the school provides little space or none, naturally see themselves as an underclass within the pupil group.

Butler's dustbins

British education has always acknowledged that these children exist. In 1944 the Butler Act tried to solve their problem by inventing the secondary modern school and sending the non-academics (assumed to be about 65-70% of the population) there to be fed a pale imitation of the grammar school curriculum, or simply corralled by teachers chosen for their skill at child-taming rather than children's learning.

Egalitarian battery houses

When the essential wrongness of this procedure dawned upon the educational establishment, the comprehensive school came into being. It swept away distinctive schools for the academic and the non-academic, and replaced them with vast, anonymous battery-houses where all sorts of egalitarian experiments could take place. They rarely did, of course, because parents and teachers alike were still mesmerised by the idea that, when all the talking and theorising was over, schools were for reading, writing and arithmetic, and any pupil who found these difficult or uninteresting needed, not an alternative curriculum, but 'remedial' teaching. Thus millions of youngsters grew up (and still grow up) believing that there is something wrong with children whose minds will not allow them to enjoy school lessons.

Right treatment, wrong disease

This is disgraceful. Imagine what would happen if doctors started saying to their patients: 'You have got the wrong disease. I am going to treat you for another disease which you haven't got, but which I enjoy treating and which makes me feel important. You really need a prescription and two days in bed, but I am highly trained in surgery, so I am going to cut you open and take something out. That is proper doctoring!'

There would be an outcry, and rightly so. Yet all over the country highly paid professionals are saying to children: 'Your skill and enthusiasms are a nuisance to us. Since you are not interested in bookwork and abstract ideas we should be allowing you to discover what you are good at. But we are not going to. Instead we shall ply you with work you cannot do well, ideas you have small chance of understanding and standards you cannot hope to rise to, and when we have finished we will blame you for your failure. That is what we call 'maintaining standards.'

We don't own them

We do this because, as a people, we have not learned that we do not own our children. It pleases us to imagine that we can commend our traditions and the accumulated culture of our nation to our children in such a way that they will maintain them in the form which we have imprinted on them. For the same reasons, we cling to the delusion that we can make our young agree with us about what is precious in music, art, and so on. We cannot, and have no right to. We may offer the next generation the undoubted riches of European culture, but we have no right to incorporate them into their lives. Whatever relative value we assign to Mozart and Heavy Metal, our superior age and experience does not entitle us to force that judgement on our children.

This is exactly what the Government is trying to do by imposing its National Curriculum on schools, sadly with the unanimous support of the Labour and Liberal Democrat parties. A succession of Conservative Secretaries of State for Education have set up working parties of teachers, academics and civil servants with a mandate to prepare a compendium of subjects which all schoolchildren will have to study. They tried to develop ideas which reflect the most recent experience and good practice in their field. Then, as often as not, their conclusions have been largely rejected, usually because they are too 'imprecise' and child-centred.

The Government, expressing its philosophy of education through the Secretary of State, has made it clear to the teaching profession that it wants children to see school-work as a celebration of high culture and traditional learning. The children are expected to imbibe it, not contribute to its development.

If they find it boring that is evidence that they need more of it, not less. The 'right' sort of child will eventually come to appreciate it, and for them all the pressure will have been worthwhile. The other sort of child, the one who obstinately refuses to see the point of learning lists of monarchs and battles, or of reading books written a century ago, will leave school a philistine, without any alternative structure of valuable ideas to sustain them through life.

Why any responsible government should want to carry on like this is hard to understand, until one examines the underlying political ideas which inform the curriculum.

Dangerous children

In any country, whatever its governing system, schools represent uncertainty and danger. They are full of new minds, freshly feeling what it is to be human, choosing priorities which, when they have come to maturity, may impel them to change their world so that it is less comfortable for their elders to live in. The next generation may even turn the world upside down and tread underfoot all their elders' ideas of vice and virtue.

For this reason governments tend to think that it is in their interest to bear down hard upon children with a stock of established ideas. If they can convince them from the beginning that only school-knowledge and approved concepts are worth anything, there is less chance that they will grow up receptive to unorthodox outlooks.

In the case of British education this concern takes the form of an obsession with reading and figuring.

A nation of clerks?

I have often been forced by my work to ask myself why maths and English have become the twin fetishes of state schooling. I am not going to suggest that they are not valuable or important in some situations. I want to know why they are the twin piles upon which all British schooling is built.

It may be that they represent for our present Government exactly the same set of priorities as moved the first curriculum managers a century ago. The purpose of schooling in those days was to ensure an adequate supply of docile employees who could read notices, rule-books and the like, and who, if need be, could do the work of a clerk or book-keeper. There is less need these days for that kind of worker, but the Government seems to feel that schoolchildren should still experience learning to read and calculate as essentially functional disciplines which are important in the National Curriculum, not for the pleasure they bring but only for the yoke which they place on the pupils' shoulders.

The pleasure principle

The truth is, of course, that maths and English, if they are to be of use to children, must be fun! If children are not learning them efficiently, it is simply because they get no pleasure from doing so. I suspect that for many children in schools throughout the country the daily round of having to show teacher how well or badly they can read and do sums, ensures that they will under-use those skills for the rest of their lives.

Unfortunately, curriculum makers, and particularly Education Ministers, have never, since the whole business of state schooling began, regarded pleasure in learning as an important consideration. The present Government is obsessed with the idea that education is a service to parents rather than children, and it clearly believes that parents will not be satisfied with schooling unless it is made harder and more irksome. As John Holt observed, they believe life is no picnic, so school should be no picnic.

To achieve their aim, Conservative Secretaries of State for Education have campaigned against every attempt which teachers have made to breathe life into the curriculum. They have repudiated what they think are child-centred methods precisely because they think they are child-centred, when in fact they are only child-referenced at the most.

This makes me wonder how supposedly serious educators can claim to be doing what is best for the nation's children.

I assume that teachers think they are preparing children to live in the adult world, where they will have to make important choices. I also assume that, as serious, thoughtful educators those teachers have worked out what they believe is the best way to achieve that goal. Therefore it is reasonable for me to ask them how their approach to educating children actually fits them for the world in which they are going to live.

Hard questions

If, for any reason, a child finds reading, writing or number-work hard to absorb, either because he or she is not mentally gifted for them, or because they lie outside the framework of the home culture, how does forcing them into children's minds against their will make it more likely that they will learn them effectively, or at all?

How does being made to learn something one is not interested in engender a desire to study it? And how does being made to behave in a certain way cause a person to adopt that behaviour as his or her own?

What evidence is there that enforcing conformity on people makes them see the value of conformity (if indeed it has any value)?

In the adult world people do work in order to earn money to live on. How does making children do 'work' for which they do not receive a penny piece give them a respect for labour?

Children learn most efficiently when they are allowed to choose when, how and for how long they study. Every one of them, whatever their performance at school, taught themselves to speak their own mother tongue, and any other languages that happened to be spoken around them, because language satisfied their need to commune with their surroundings and because they had complete freedom to work out its structure for themselves. In contrast to that success, many pupils are bored at school and fail to grasp the subjects which they study even at the simplest levels. Is this because they are stupid, or is it because their studies meet no intellectual need which they happen to have?

Why do we accept, generation after generation, that after all our striving to get them interested in the richness of our national culture many children will leave school determined never to read, write or calculate seriously again?

Schooling is compulsory for most children. If a thing is compulsory and it fails, is that not a crying injustice?

The myth takes over

An institution based on essentially fascist thinking about the curriculum will not address itself to these questions. It will avoid thinking about the impact which it has on individual children because it assumes that individuals have little significance or none. Only the life of the mass community counts. Its rulers will naturally use schooling to inculcate the myths from which the nation derives its image of itself and of its place in the world.

It is worth pointing out here that 'myth' is not a word which implies deception. Every nation in the ancient world created and passed on to its posterity special stories. They were recognised as fiction—often extravagant fiction about gods, heroes, and journeys through enchanted lands. But the people who heard these stories revered them because they saw in them deep truths about their origins and the glory they aspired to, preserved in allegory and symbol. They entertained, but they also inspired. The people to whom they belonged recognised in them the venerable dreams of their ancestors, and felt strengthened by them. The truth which the stories contained was not in their events but in the emotions which they enabled their hearers to feel. The Greeks called them 'mythoi'.

In the twentieth century it might seem that myths no longer work. In fact, they are still vibrantly alive, and through the curriculum the school ensures that they continue to govern the nation's most fundamental thinking and feeling.

Of course, we no longer look much to heroes for inspiration. Our national mythology concerns itself more with describing the type and level of culture which expresses our 'true' character. So we lay before our children a curriculum which in essence says this about us as a people: ' The British are a great people because they always accept the need to do unpleasant things with a good grace.

In pursuit for their mania for difficult, boring tasks to do they value calculation far above mathematics. Though every child has access to an electronic calculator, schools set set great store by the learning of multiplication tables. This severely limits the time spent learning and appreciating the great ideas about numbers and their relationships which have made this century such an interesting time to live in. This is rather regrettable, perhaps, but not really important, since children do not go to school to have their private interests catered for.

For similar reasons they load their children with anxiety about the spelling system which English has developed. This is hard to learn, illogical and even downright silly sometimes, but children have to master it, suppressing the temptation to use their own phonetic alternative spellings, before anything they write can be taken seriously and appreciated for its content rather than its form.

They love their past, and live in its shadow, reminding their children endlessly of how their Great Men (and a small number of Great Women) led armies recruited from the common people to trample over other countries, crushing their inhabitants and exploiting them. This turned out to be a good thing for the conquered, because when the British had brought them under the yoke they taught them how to be cheap imitations of the English, with half-British names, British clothes, babu accents and the quaint belief that their true homeland was England.

They think of themselves as exceptionally devoted to fair play and justice. They tell their young that English people help old ladies across the street, give up their seats in buses to pensioners, never hit females and tell the truth at all times. None of these delicacies apply to children, who are explicitly shut out from the normal community because they are too young to have social value, except as love-objects and dressing dolls. They must expect to be hit, lied to, shoved aside without warning or good reason. Above all, they must never express their feelings or expect that adults will take them seriously.

The English believe their children need what they call a 'balanced curriculum'. This simply means a set of lessons which cover knowledge from both the scientific and the artistic sides of human experience. The aim of this is supposed to be to give children an experience of all types of knowledge. It is noticeable, however, that even when they have a reasonable time to decide which bits of the curriculum interest them and which do not, pupils still have to study them all.

If you doubt, as I am sure many readers do, whether this is a true representation of what schools are trying to put over to their pupils, ask yourself why so many folk in Britain are enthusiastic about the National Curriculum and the system of standard testing which the Conservative Government has been so determined to introduce, and why Government ministers have been so grimly intent upon re-establishing in schools the primacy of old texts, classical ideas about literature and music, old-fashioned mathematics, (in other words, sums that parents can do as well as their children), and prescriptive teaching by which teachers tell children what they have to learn instead of allowing them to explore knowledge in their own way.

Ask yourself also why so many adults who are involved with education, as teachers or administrators become angry when anyone suggests to them that the prescriptive curriculum, forced upon all children in the name of 'equal opportunity' is actually the cause of ignorance and philistinism in society, rather than the cure. The reason cannot be that they have analysed the alternative methods and found them wanting. Neither can it be that they remember how good their own education was. I have often heard the same adult denounce modern child-centred methods of teaching in one breath, and in the next describe how boring and useless their own schooling was.

The culture of hardness revisited

Perhaps their true motivation was summed up for me by a colleague of mine some years ago. I had been talking to her about the grey, strained expressions I saw on the faces of my pupils as they went about the school. I suggested that it might be something to do with their feeling that they were not being educated so much as sentenced to hard labour for the crime of being children. She thought for a moment, and said in a grim voice: 'I went through it. I see no reason why my child should escape.'

Knowledge worth having?

The people who compiled the National Curriculum seem to have a clear idea of what knowledge is worth having. I do not know how they arrived at it. Probably they assumed that the knowledge they happened to possess was valuable because it was theirs, and by making children struggle to learn it they could impose upon the next generation the broad scheme of values they themselves cherished. These people seem to believe that nothing has educational value unless it leads to a test of some sort, designed to prove that the pupil has at least been made to submit to the study of this supposedly 'valuable' knowledge. The pleasure of adding to one's understanding, satisfying one's curiosity or simply doing something enjoyable have no place in their model of education.

Cheated twice over

The result of this thinking is that schools are full of children who do not enjoy or value their study. Neither when they are at school, nor at any time in their future lives do they experience any of the 'enrichment' which their parents were led to believe they were receiving in exchange for the endless hours of schooling they had to endure. The 'balance' and 'breadth' of their curriculum, its 'structure' and 'rigour' never do them any good that they can discern. They are doubly cheated: it forces them to work at subjects which they cannot absorb because they are not interested, and it deprives them of any chance to find what they are good at and pursue it seriously.

Unable to compete in the battle for jobs some of them settle down to a life of unemployment, punctuated by casual labour and opportunistic crime. Thus they find their way inevitably to the social level where their main purpose is to provide police, social workers and lawyers with a staple source of work.

We must stop using the curriculum as a social stratifier. We owe our children a duty to see that they emerge from school not, as they are now, divided into qualified people—their social worthiness measured by their success in grasping a limited range of ideas chosen for them by the Government—and a swelling underclass without merits or prospects.

Chapter six

Under occupation

For as long as there have been schools adults have been telling each other why children behave badly in them. Painted with a broad brush the explanation goes like this:

'School is good and necessary for children. Good children realise that and settle down to work. Bad children do not. They are insolent, lazy, noisy and obstructive. This makes it hard for everybody to teach them the important things which we adults know they need to learn. Therefore it is very important that teachers take them in hand and force them to do as they are told. Any teacher who cannot or will not is a weakling and should be hounded out of the profession.'

I have rarely heard anyone offer an alternative explanation for the difficult conduct of some schoolchildren, and I suspect that for all practical purposes it is the only one normal people understand. I believe it is wrong, and based on a concept of what children are which has, for many centuries, legitimised and justified oppression.

For freedom

I believe that children who disrupt school are not bad people, but rather healthy young minds displaying something like the spirit which drove the French resistance to stand against the German occupier. The Maquis were, of course, adults, and their enemies were ruthless, mechanised troops ready to kill, torture and deport the inhabitants of occupied countries. That should not blind us to the fact that the chief reason why Frenchmen went out at night to ambush the Germans and destroy their installations was not primarily that they were cruel, but simply that they were there, issuing orders and enforcing control over people who had not chosen to be ruled by them.

Even the most benevolent, sensitive dictatorship cries out to be overthrown if it has seized power by force against the wishes of the people. The argument that it governs them better, or is more 'progressive' than any native regime has, rightly, come to be seen as a discredited part of the substructure of imperialism. We no longer accept that anyone has the right to go into a neighbour's country and run it for them just because the invader is more 'civilised' and 'advanced' than the victim. If anyone does, we take the side of the invaded people without a second thought, and praise them for their courage.

We did that when the Soviets invaded Afghanistan. The Western nations showered the 'brave Mujahedin' with high-tech weapons, and our collective heart leapt with jubilation when the Red Army withdrew. We neither knew or cared that the Soviet-backed regime had provided modern medical and social services for the Afghans and largely wiped out the traditional ill-treatment of women.

Our instinct—a healthy one, in my opinion—is to believe that no inequality between the civilisation or culture of two nations can ever entitle one nation to assume guardianship over the other.

Adult imperialism

Yet every day we take children under our adult wing and impose on them a way of life which strikes many of them as little different from being under occupation. We decide what they will wear, how and when they will study, what time they will go out and come in, in fact almost every detail of their lives. If they obey us and fit in with our plans, well and good: we allow them to live what remains of their lives largely unhindered. They are no danger to us, so we do not bear down on them heavily. As long as they concede our dominance we can allow ourselves to smile on them. If on the other hand they decide to reject our efforts to administer their lives for them they become a real danger to us. They challenge both our adult ideas about how life is to be ordered and our right to force each successive generation into adopting them.

I have no doubt that in their occupation of France in the Second World War, the Germans took the view, as every other occupier has done since the dawn of time, that: 'We are here now and ours is the responsibility to maintain order at whatever cost. The oppressive things we have to do are regrettable but necessary if we are to keep the wheels of ordinary life turning and the essential machinery of the state working smoothly. We cannot let scruples divert us from the task in hand. Those who sabotage us are bandits and scoundrels who want to sweep aside all decent order and drag us into chaos. They must be crushed.'

It is easy for us to take a similar stance in education. Of course we do not actually use those words when we talk about difficult children in the school culture—though I have heard, on more than one occasion, teachers refer to pupils as the enemy. Yet the ferocity with which some teachers react to dissident behaviour from school students makes me, for one, suspect that behind the professional mask they feel little different from soldiers in an occupied country.

Their fierceness is understandable, of course. They feel like the children's enemy. If that sounds melodramatic or exaggerated, it is worth looking at some of the basic behaviours which are almost universal among schoolchildren, and asking whether they resemble more closely the attitude of eager learners to benevolent educators, or that of conquered people to their conquerors.

The first casualty

Truth is the first casualty. In all my years of teaching I have never found myself in a school where children thought it was safe or reasonable to tell the truth to an adult. Children learn to lie because it is the only way to be safe and to protect their fellow pupils. Worse, they discover very quickly that adults expect them to lie, and do not believe anything they say. From this they deduce that any adult who does believe them is either profoundly stupid or dangerously naive. I have tried over the years to treat children as potentially honest citizens, by believing what they say to me, and I have often heard them say: 'You didn't really believe us, did you? How silly!' In this way youngsters come to have less and less confidence in honesty and truth-telling as the basis of human relationships.

For us or against us?

The purpose for which children come to school is usually described as education. Education is surely a benign thing, in which children and adults ought to co-operate. What goes on in many schools is something else: a war in which both sides cling to the solidarity of their group as if all depended on it. The result is that, against all reason, pupils close their ranks to protect each other against teachers, and teachers do the same to ensure that they are always seen to be in the right. *Omertà*, the unbreakable rule of silence which protects Mafiosi from justice and keeps oppressed people all over the world under the yoke, operates with full vigour in school. Pupils dare not tell their teachers that they are being bullied, or that some other pupil has stolen from them because they would be stigmatised as traitors. In the same way, they could never allow themselves to challenge openly the disruptive pupil who ruins lessons. Universal schooling has simply taught them, as it has taught everyone since it began, that schools are run on paper by the head teacher and the staff, but in fact by the Law of the Jungle.

The culture of the oppressed

In more recent years this unrecognised but pernicious state of affairs has grown another, no less diseased offshoot. People of my age tend to react with despair to the culture of fashion and pop music which grips young people, but I suspect that if we had had enough money when we were young to keep up with the vertiginous round of new clothing styles and chart-topping records we would have been as enthusiastic about it as youngsters are today, because it is, I am convinced, the equivalent of native culture in an occupied country. I suspect that many children are attracted to pop culture less by the charm of its raucous music and ever-changing couture, and more by the rebellion against adult values which it represents.

So powerfully does pop culture identify its devotees as members of an oppressed group that in many schools pupils attack any child who has not been able to get fashionable clothes or keep up with changes in style, as if he or she were a traitor. I remember asking a young friend of mine why on earth he had saved up to buy what looked to me like a rather nondescript T-shirt with a fashionable label for £50. I thought he had been monstrously overcharged, but another youngster gave me the reason. 'It's better than being beaten up in the playground!' he said.

Why so blind?

I am at a loss to know why adult society has not recognised how serious this situation is. We expect young people to reject, in part at least, the staid cultural traditions of their elders, and we accept that the vacuous claptrap of popular music and fashion serve as a safe enclosure in which the young people work out for themselves what they wish to become as an adult. However when youth culture becomes the badge and uniform by which young people distinguish friends (worthwhile people who can be cared for and helped) from traitors (whom it is a duty to despise and hurt in any way possible) it has taken on an altogether new and dangerous character.

If, as I believe, the roots of spurious youth culture lie in schools, the sooner schools begin to ask themselves why children absorb it so easily and hold to it so tenaciously, the better for us all. After all, the Government spends millions of pounds every year on plying our children with what is sees as the best of our national culture. It pays for teachers to learn things which it wants to pass on to the next generation, and it specifies in great detail what shall and shall not be taught in schools. It clearly believes that by doing this it can ensure that more and more youngsters become accustomed to reading good literature, listening to good music, writing well-structured English and revelling in the elegance of higher mathematics. Yet when they leave school young people in the main reject aggressively all that stuff and throw themselves into the kaleidoscopic round of discos and fashion-chasing. I should have thought that failure on such a grand scale deserves at least a Royal Commission.

My experience suggests to me that the antipathy of some children to Authority's plans for their lives is so great that it generates an anger which distorts their perspectives of even the most reasonable aspects of school life.

B goes to War

I remember many years ago teaching in a school run by a man who had been an army officer in wartime. He saw his school as just another regiment, and yearned to see all his teachers controlling their pupils like non-commissioned officers at Catterick or Aldershot. One of his favourite teachers held firmly to the 'good old methods'. 'I wish we all had B's discipline' he used to sigh at staff meetings when the evergreen subject of behaviour came up. I, for my part, wished I had the courage to tell him what I thought of B's discipline, because I had seen a different side of it from him.

One day I was walking down the corridor, past B's class-room, when she saw me and called out: 'Mr Shute! I'd like to talk to you.' I stopped and she swept out of the room with a monitory glance at the children. No sooner had she left their range of vision than a feral howl burst from every child's throat. I have rarely heard such a sudden, concentrated and frightening outburst of noise. I want to emphasise that I am not embroidering a tale that happens to favour my point of view. I have chosen my words very carefully and I mean every one of them. Those children were angry. She went back at once and quelled them, but no sooner had she left them a second time than the din broke out again, even louder this time. She gave up trying to speak to me and concentrated on making the class pay for its temerity.

B's discipline was also a cause of trouble to me. I had a class of pleasant, intelligent children every week for French. Four of our meetings were as pleasant as any lesson could be in a traditional school, but the fifth... Every Friday they came in boiling, and I could not even start the lesson until I had brought them under control, which often took half the lesson. Baffled by this strange pattern of events, I tried to discover the reason for it. Since I had them in hand at other times, I doubted if my liberal approach to teaching was much to blame. I could only surmise that it was something to do with what they had been doing before my lesson. I consulted the timetable, and was not much surprised to find that they had just had forty minutes under B's all-seeing eye.

I imagine B, if I had had the temerity to tackle her about this problem, would have said that hers was the proper discipline, and it was my job not to oppose her but to take up the torch she had lit and keep it burning. I could not, of course. I cannot bring myself to see education as she saw it—a life-long campaign against spontaneity, liveliness, and the natural energy of youth. Neither can I accept that the anger and frustration I saw in those children, which I now recognise as the same anger felt by slaves and occupied people, serves any good purpose in education.

If we had really imbibed the humanism on which we claim to base our national life we should have the courage to confront the anger of our children fearlessly and begin to remove the things which cause it. We should understand that when children show they are hurt by our well-meaning attempts to 'educate' them, the pain they feel is as authentic as that which adults suffer when their lives are disrupted by war, disease or bereavement.

Chapter Seven

Alice Miller and the mental abuse of children

Like most teachers—indeed, the vast majority of adults—I used to accept that, dangerous and stupid though it seemed, the commonly accepted way of relating to children was the only one available to me. It certainly made children angry and difficult to talk to as fellow human beings, but their attitude seemed 'natural', and since I was unable to assign a cause to it for many years I worked on the assumption that the best I could hope for was to moderate the more corrosive parts of it in my classroom, and hope that the general trend in society towards a more liberal, permissive way of life would finally transform even our attitudes towards children.

Then I began to read Alice Miller. Dr. Miller, a German-speaking child psychotherapist, illuminated my limited understanding of children through her books. I read *For your own good* (published by Virago) and it brought about a revolution in my thinking.

The book deals with what she calls, graphically, 'poisonous pedagogy', the systematic and well-nigh universal practice of forcing children to hide their feelings, especially their reactions, when their parents bear down upon them with parental discipline in most of its traditional forms. She quotes at length from German books on child-rearing which emphasise that in order to bring their children up 'properly' parents must concentrate all their efforts on making sure that, from the very beginning of their lives the youngsters never come to place their emotional needs above those of the parents. This is an inflexible rule, hammered home time after time in these supposedly learned manuals of 'good' parenting.

Murderous parenting

Alice Miller traces the awful results of this repression in the lives of such people as Jurgen Bartsch, a young child-murderer, who was himself beaten and abused by his loveless parents, and Adolf Hitler, whose father beat him frequently, and whistled to call him as if he were a dog. In both these cases Dr. Miller analyses clearly the way in which the childhood suffering of Bartsch and Hitler generated their murderous behaviour in later life. She recognises that traditional psychotherapy does not supply a true evaluation of the pathology of violence because it assumes, as Freud himself did, that violent impulses are the result of thwarted drives.

The traditional view was that these drives come from within the individual, and are part of his or her innate mental structure. Problems arose, the traditionalists taught, when the individual did not succeed in dealing appropriately with these drives.

Dr. Miller rejected the drive theory because in later life she was helped by a sympathetic art therapist to see that she had herself had been emotionally abused as a child. She had forgotten all about the experience, and it was only when she allowed herself to relive it that she understood how it had moulded her thinking about the origins of human behaviour and her relationships with her clients. She realised that drive theory was simply a smokescreen behind which the very people who elaborated it were hiding from the reality of their own experience.

'My parents, right or wrong'

It began with Freud. In his efforts to understand why his patients were seized with destructive, violent impulses he looked at their early life. He found, as you might expect, memories of harsh, aloof parents, loneliness, and emotional pressure, but he could not, by his own admission, bring himself to blame those parents. Like the great majority of his contemporaries he accepted that a person must always honour his or her father and mother, however they chose to treat them.

Seen, but not heard

The natural response to being abused is to resent, and if possible to strike back at the abuser. Dr. Miller realised that children were uniquely disqualified by their age, physical development and social status from effectively expressing their true feelings. If their parents hit them, or used other oppressive methods to 'discipline' them they might cry or throw a tantrum, but this generally earned them more and more painful punishment. They soon learned that it was safest to keep their indignation and despair to themselves.

In this children were denied their natural reaction. Very early in their lives they generally learned that their feelings, whatever they might be, had no status at all in the world. They must suppress them, shut them away, keep them out of sight. Sooner or later, they had to forget them, and adjust their minds to the point where it enabled them to share with their parents a conviction that they had no right to be angry about any aspect of their lives, however painful.

Analyst, know thyself

The impact of this discovery on Dr. Miller's thinking was volcanic. She began to suspect that not only were children's problems not being cured by traditional methods of psychoanalysis, but that the analysts themselves—because they had failed to confront and express their anguish and indignation about the abuse they had suffered in their own childhood—systematically closed to their patients the one path down which they might have found the truth about their pain. The analysts refused to allow their clients to confront the many times in childhood when they had wanted to receive warmth, love, understanding and respect from their parents, and got instead 'discipline'.

The eleventh Commandment: 'Thou shalt forget'

From this insight, Dr. Miller went on to discover that the collective amnesia which she had perceived among the analysts was more widespread. She found that it also pervaded the media. She wrote articles about her discoveries and found that they were either refused or edited so severely that they no longer conveyed her message. A television programme about her work was constructed in such a way that its serious impact was largely lost under a tide of musical interludes and distracting short items. She was struggling against an almost universal assumption that children do not suffer when their feelings are thwarted or when their parents treat them harshly. Indeed, it became clear to her that most adults saw children as insensately demanding little Visigoths who, given half a chance, would swarm over their parents' defences and despoil them of everything which made life worth living. This belief, she insisted, was engendered by the very pain it sought to deny. Generation after generation of abused children forgot their suffering, transformed it into 'good, firm discipline' and visited it upon their own children.

The perpetual arena

I offer no apology for invoking Dr. Miller's name in the context of a book about the fascist tendency in schooling, because I have come to the conclusion that her ideas explain, clearly and boldly, why our schools are often such barren places. Quite simply, they furnish their teachers, and the parents of their pupils, with an arena in which the adults can enact upon the bodies and minds of the pupils the suffering which they endured when they themselves were young. I believe this is the unrecognised motivation which gives rise to all fascism, both the microcosmic fascism of the classroom, and the great political disease of the twentieth century.

Painful truth

This is not pleasant, and it will not be well received. Teachers naturally want to present their dealings with children as careful, professional, and stemming from a mature assessment of what is necessary to achieve successful education. Parents in their turn desperately hope to be known as 'good' parents. For the reasons I have just mentioned, 'good' parents are generally assumed to be the ones who tolerate no dissent or disrespect from their children, and who have no difficulty in making them obey. Therefore, in saying what I have said I have almost certainly aroused in some of my readers an *odium theologicum* as intense as their own upbringing was harsh, and as deep as the mental vaults in which they have hidden their memory of it.

I apologise to them all, not for offending them (the decision to be offended or not lies in each individual's hands), but for confronting them with a truth which they cannot easily live with because they have spent a lifetime evading it. I am speaking of the truth that in our Western society child abuse is not an isolated aberration: it is normal. It happens to the children of every generation. They grow into adults, and when they have children of their own they transform the hidden agony of their early years into a conviction that those children 'need' to be kept under firm control.

In this way they show that they have never been able to confront their own anger at being themselves controlled. Instead, they have forgotten it, to the point where its very intensity contributes to the mechanism which keeps it hidden! Unable to allow themselves to face the fact that their parents treated them badly they make a virtue of re-enacting that bad treatment as if it were the best possible way to bring children up.

Training or abuse?

I accept that few adults, even of the more liberal sort, would think of the normal behaviour of parents towards children as abusive. Beyond excessive physical harshness and sexual interference, which we have at last come to recognise as evil, we assume that it is all right for grown-ups to do, or not do, almost anything which takes their fancy in training their children. Our culture encourages them to feel that they are entitled to deem anything their youngster does to be 'naughty' and punish him or her for it, disregarding any confused, fearful thoughts the child may have on the subject. We allow parents to feel that they always know exactly what is going on inside their child's mind. As a result, they need have no compunction about reproving or punishing him or her for behaviours which come not from a wish to do wrong, but only from an honest misunderstanding of the complex world in which adults force them to live.

We must break the cycle

If we are ever going to change our national ethos so that it tends to favour a more democratic way of life for all citizens I am convinced one thing is essential. We must break into the cycle which begins with angry, thwarted children and ends with violent adults who cannot feel the anguish which they routinely inflict on the generation which comes after them. We must find a way to convince them that if that generation grows up poisoned, they, and they alone, are to blame.

Chapter eight

What is to be done?

School is for children

To begin with we must campaign against compulsory schooling, urgently and resolutely. At present the Government sees schools as a service to parents. They are not. They are a service to children and to no-one else. If children have to be dragged to them by so-called 'welfare officers' the schools are clearly failing those children. Instead of branding absentees with the title of 'truant' (originally a mediaeval French bandit!) schools ought to be asking why their clients don't want what they offer. If schools do not ask this question they are without excuse, like any other public institution which does not do efficiently what its clients need it to do. If a hospital does not cure its patients it closes and its staff get the sack. The same principle should govern schools. If they don't make their pupils happy, contented, lively and responsible they should close and their teachers do something more in harmony with their talents (running a prison perhaps).

When we have freed children from having to attend school whether they want to or not, we must go on to strip away from schools the clap-trap which prevents the human beings within them from meeting each other's needs. The national curriculum, with its lunatic insistence upon delivering to all pupils the same arbitrary parcel of subjects, must be replaced by a stock of resources built up in response to what the pupils feel they need to learn.

This cannot happen while the children have no voice in the school. Therefore the school must be run by all the people who share its facilities, either as paid teachers, volunteers, domestics, caterers, pupils or visitors with special skills to impart. A school in which adults bore children with compulsory teaching they do not want and never find any use for in later life must be seen for the nonsense it is. Just as we would be shocked to hear of a doctor who bled children to cure them, or a builder who used wattle and daub instead of bricks, we must learn to be amazed by the idea of schools holding compulsory lessons which all children have to attend, whatever the cast of their minds.

School must become the natural place for children to go with their energy, their full-hearted enjoyment of activity, their love of new experiences. They must go to school knowing that when they arrive sympathetic people will allow them to do whatever is in the forefront of their minds until they have drawn from it all the interest it holds for them, provided only that it harms no-one else. There must be places where they can be quiet, and places where they can make all the noise they want to.

We must allow them to judge for themselves how long they pursue any activity. The idea that you always have to finish the thing you start is a grown up one and it has to do with the payment workers get for completing their allotted work. If we want children to make a virtue of never leaving things undone we must have the good grace to pay them for what they do. Children only finish activities if they are interesting and worthwhile. It is absurd to make a youngster struggle on to complete an exercise or whatever else he or she is doing when it no longer grips his or her mind. The only way to make such an activity maintain its grasp its to pay for it to be done. I recognise that this is probably the most Quixotic statement I have made so far, but it is right.

A place where truth can be told

Our school—let's call it the Really Useful School—must have a forum where any person of any age can say in safety anything he or she wants to say. They must, of course, be prepared to take the natural consequences of hurting others' feelings, which is generally to be told that they cannot abuse others with impunity. There must be a clearly understood system for settling disputes between people who use the school, teachers and pupils alike. It must be founded on the assumption that all have the same right to have their feelings considered.

Off with its Head!

Since head teachers tend to have a vested interest in their schools becoming easy places to govern-which usually means creating a place of more-or-less benevolent fascism in which what the staff say goes-it is hard to imagine their continuing to be necessary. The head's function is anomalous anyway. The head is unlikely to be promoted in the present system unless able to show that he or she can direct successfully an enterprise as large and complex as a school in a preordained direction, suppressing, when necessary, any subordinate with markedly different ideas. In the Really Useful School, dissidence, questioning and unpredictability will be the order of the day. It follows that if there is to be a head he or she must be a person who can work against everything a conventional head values, a person able to discern when staff and pupils are losing their nerve and adopting old-fashioned, simplistic solutions to the problems of freedom. Above all, he or she must have the courage to resist parents when they begin to worry because their child hasn't reached Blue Book Five, or hasn't been given homework.

For what it may be worth, I think that when a school-community begins to work in the way I have outlined it tends to be capable of doing for itself everything a head does in the traditional school. If the pupils know that they have to account to the school meeting for their actions, they will be less tempted to think of rule-breaking as a skirmish in the war against authority. Instead of deferring to a single charismatic individual, who may be a fearsome presence as he or she moves about the school, pupils at the Really Useful School will learn that the community is the supreme authority. They will learn to obey its laws because they helped to shape them, and they will learn that it is everywhere, in every pupil and adult. Unlike the old-fashioned head teacher the school-community does not set itself apart from everybody in an office hedged around with marks of special prestige. It is effective and serviceable because it does not have to guess what people think and feel: it knows because it constantly hears them expressing their point of view, and can react in the best way

'Who are you to give us orders?'

The aim of the school must be to cultivate a critical attitude towards authority. At present children mostly leave school either imbued with a submissive deference to authority or determined to flout it. A submissive population will readily accept the rule of anyone endowed with the right combination of demagogy and ruthlessness. The knee-jerk dissidents will not be able to distinguish between reasonable rules and arbitrary authority. The result will be more-or-less what exists today: an easily manipulable majority and a dissident fringe so fragmented that their message is ignored. What we need are young people who can discern the difference between authority which protects the proper interests of some part of society, and authority which has no power but sustaining those who possess it.

You are not required to finish the work ...

I accept, as anyone writing this kind of work must, that I am struggling against a vast, complacent establishment which feels no need to reform. The government, whatever its colour, knows that there are few votes to be gained from any programme which involves 'going soft' on children. The old methods have gained an ascendancy over the common mind. However carefully argued and cogent their arguments, the non-liberals only have to state the autocratic position and most ordinary observers assume that they, and not the liberals, have won.

... but you may not abstain from doing it (the Talmud)

The tragedy of our society, potentially the most humane and progressive there has ever been, is that most of its members want the education of their children to be simple, robust, no-nonsense, and as much like their own as possible. Good education, education that enlivens and empowers the child for the rest of his or her life is the opposite of that. It is full of questioning, probing and speculation. It abounds in false starts, mistakes and unfinished experiments. It values the child as he or she is now, not as the adult one would like him or her to become. It is perilous because it cannot be assessed by any reliable system of tests: you cannot examine happiness, or give a mark out of ten for inventiveness or clarity of thought. Above all, it leads to independence of mind, and instinctively the established adult world hates and fears independent thinking, especially in children.

Yet we are obligated to change our system of education so that it respects and nurtures its pupils, opening their minds and setting free their spirits. We are obligated by the millions murdered obediently by well-schooled 'civilised' white Europeans, by the very experience of having lived through the most homicidal century there has ever been, and by the love we owe to the humans who have not yet been born, of whose happiness we hold the key. We like to think we have already almost arrived at that state of affairs. In fact, I believe, we have not even started the journey.

Publisher's postscript

Only *education* is compulsory!

Schooling is **not** compulsory in the United Kingdom—except by popular misconception. In the UK it is **education** that is compulsory for children. In law, parents have a basic choice: they can educate their children either by sending them to school or 'otherwise', using a home-based programme.

In law these two choices are absolute rights. There is a third possibility. It is a flexi-time arrangement: part-time school-based, part home-based. As yet this is not an absolute right and is therefore open to the veto of a school or a local education authority. Nevertheless a few families have succeeded in negotiating a flexi-time programme with a local school.

Since parents are not informed of their rights—an obvious place would have been the Parents' Charter—most believe that schooling is compulsory in the UK and act on this erroneous assumption.

In the UK, USA and elsewhere, the steady growth of home-based education is something of a quiet revolution, increasing in the UK from a handful of families to about 5000 in the last ten years. In the USA one and a half million families are now operating home-based education programmes. The research shows them to be very successful in achieving their chosen aims.

Two organisations exist to give support to families opting for home based education. They are:

Education Otherwise, 36 Kinross Road, Leamington Spa CV32 7EF

Children's Home-based Education Association (CHEA) 14 Basil Avenue, Armthorpe, Doncaster DN3 2AR

A useful book, *Learning from home based education* is available, price £5, from Education Now, 113 Arundel Drive, Bramcote Hills, Nottingham NG9 3FQ. Cheques should be made payable to 'Education Now'.